Alligators
and
Crocodiles!
Strange and Wonderful

Laurence Pringle

Illustrated by Meryl Henderson

BOYDS MILLS PRESS

HONESDALE, PENNSYLVANIA

For Roger Williamson, a friend of the Highlights Foundation, who enjoys
spending time and energy in helping others succeed as children's authors
—L.P.

The author wishes to thank James Perran Ross, Ph.D., Executive Office, Crocodile Specialist Group, Florida Museum of Natural History, University of Florida, and Kent A. Vliet, Ph.D., Coordinator of Laboratories, Biological Science Program, Department of Zoology, University of Florida, for reviewing the text and illustrations of this book for accuracy.

Text copyright © 2009 by Laurence Pringle
Illustrations copyright © 2009 by Meryl Henderson

Boyds Mills Press
815 Church Street
Honesdale, Pennsylvania 18431
Printed in China
www.boydsmillspress.com

Library of Congress Cataloging-in-Publication Data

Pringle, Laurence P.
  Alligators and crocodiles! : strange and wonderful / by Laurence Pringle ; illustrated by Meryl Henderson. — 1st ed.
     p. cm.
  ISBN 978-1-59078-256-9 (hardcover : alk. paper)
  1. Alligators—Juvenile literature. 2. Crocodiles—Juvenile literature. I. Henderson, Meryl, ill. II. Title.
  QL666.C925P75 2009
  597.98—dc22
                                      2008030018

First edition, 2009

The text of this book is set in 15-point Clearface.
The illustrations are done in watercolor.

10 9 8 7 6 5 4 3 2 1

Erk, erk, erk. Erk, erk, erk, erk.

Baby alligators called to their mother. They called from inside their eggs, which she had buried within a mound of grasses and other plants. For more than two months the mother alligator had guarded the eggs in their nest. Now about forty baby alligators were ready to hatch.

Erk, erk, erk, the babies called. Where was their mother?

She heard their voices and hurried to the nest. With her claws she raked away the decaying plants that covered the eggs.

Erk, erk, erk, the baby alligators called. Some had already hatched. They first had to cut through a tough membrane with a special egg tooth on their snouts, then they pushed against the shell with their heads. Others were still trying to break free.

The mother alligator picked up one of these eggs with her mouth. Her teeth and jaws were strong enough to break animal bones and crush turtle shells, but she held the egg gently. With her tongue she rolled it against the roof of her mouth until the shell cracked open. She let the hatchling wriggle out of her mouth, then picked up another unhatched egg.

When all of her young were free of their eggs, the mother alligator crawled away from the nest. She carried some young in her mouth. Other little ones followed. She led them to the water's edge. The hatchlings swam, but they stayed close to their mother. Some rested on her back. For many weeks she would guard her young from danger.

The Spanish words el lagarto *mean "the lizard."*
These words, spoken by Spanish explorers of
America, led to the name alligator.

Mother alligator helps
her babies hatch.

5

Few people know that mother alligators give tender care to their young. In this and other ways, alligators act like birds. Alligators call to one another, lay eggs in nests, and guard their young. However, alligators are not birds. They are part of a special group of reptiles called crocodilians.

These reptiles are called crocodilians because more than half of this reptile group are called crocodiles. Of the other crocodilians, five are caimans, two are alligators, and one is a gharial.

Sarcosuchus imperator

Indopacific crocodile

Cuvier's dwarf caiman

Crocodilians are Earth's biggest living reptiles. Even the smallest kind—Cuvier's dwarf caiman—grows to be five feet long. The biggest—Indopacific crocodiles—can reach a length of more than twenty-three feet.

Today's biggest crocodilians are dwarfed by some of their ancient ancestors. Scientists have discovered fossil skeletons of crocodile-like animals that lived more than two hundred million years ago. One that lived more than a hundred million years ago was named *Sarcosuchus imperator*. Its skull alone was more than six feet long. Its total body, head to tail, was about thirty-six feet long (as long as a big school bus). From studying this crocodile's jaws and teeth, scientists believe that *Sarcosuchus* ate big animals, including large fish and dinosaurs.

Crocodilians lived on Earth *before* dinosaurs and *during* the time of dinosaurs. What's more, when dinosaurs died out about sixty-five million years ago, crocodilians lived on *after* the dinosaurs. Today crocodilians can still be found in some of Earth's warmest climates. Fourteen species of crocodiles are shown on the following six pages.

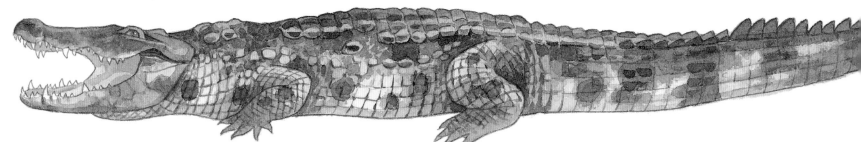

American Crocodile
Up to 20 feet long, this is the most widespread crocodile in the Americas. It lives in southern Florida, some Caribbean islands, Mexico, and central and northern South America.

Dwarf Crocodile
One of the smallest crocodilians, reaching about 6 feet in length, this species lives in western and central Africa.

Nile Crocodile
The most widespread of all African crocodiles, the Nile crocodile can grow up to 20 feet. Scientists now believe there are two kinds of Nile crocodile—one in central and West Africa, the other in East Africa and Madagascar.

Cuban Crocodile
Found only in parts of Cuba, this crocodile grows to about 12 feet.

African Slender-Snouted Crocodile
Living in central and western Africa, this is a medium-sized crocodile, reaching about 13 feet in length.

Morelet's Crocodile
This small crocodile—about 10 feet long—lives in parts of eastern Mexico, Belize, and Guatemala.

Orinoco Crocodile
Named for the South American river in which it lives, this crocodile sometimes grows to be 20 feet long.

Philippine Crocodile
Growing to no more than 10 feet, this species
is found only on some Philippine islands.

Siamese Crocodile
About 13 feet long, this crocodile lives in Thailand, Vietnam, and
other parts of Southeast Asia.

New Guinea Crocodile
Living in parts of New Guinea,
north of Australia, this crocodile
sometimes grows to be 13 feet long.

Indopacific Crocodile
Often called the saltwater crocodile or "saltie," this is
the biggest of all crocodilians, growing as long as 23 feet.
It is widespread through Asia and the western Pacific.

Mugger Crocodile
Up to 13 feet long, the mugger, or marsh, crocodile lives in parts of India, Pakistan, and Sri Lanka.

Johnston's Crocodile
About 10 feet long, this species—also called the Australian freshwater crocodile—lives in northern Australia.

False Gharial
This reptile's long, slender snout looks like that of a gharial, but its other characteristics lead herpetologists (scientists who study reptiles and amphibians) to consider it a kind of crocodile. It grows to about 13 feet in length and lives in parts of Thailand, Borneo, and Sumatra.

Like all reptiles, crocodilians are cold-blooded. This means that their body temperature depends mostly on the temperature of their surroundings. They often lie in the open where sunlight warms their bodies. To cool off, they move into a shady place or slip underwater. Sometimes they rest with wide-open mouths so that heat leaves their bodies. Crocodilians live where the water stays warm all year long. Only alligators are able to survive in cool climates. In the winter, waters sometimes turn icy in the Carolinas and other northern areas where American alligators live.

American Alligator
Found in the southeastern United States from southern Virginia to eastern Texas, this alligator can grow to be 15½ feet long.

Chinese Alligator
About half as long, at most, as the American alligator, this species survives only in a small area of China's lower Yangtze River.

Common Caiman
Up to 8 feet long, the common caiman has a vast range in South America and lives as far north as southern Mexico.

Gharial

One of the most ancient of all crocodilians, the gharial
lives in northern India, Pakistan, Nepal, and Bangladesh.
It can reach a length of 21 feet.

Schneider's Dwarf Caiman

Living in small streams of the Amazon and Orinoco regions of
South America, this species sometimes grows to a length of 6 feet.

Broad-Snouted Caiman

Living in parts of eastern Brazil, Uruguay, and Argentina, this
crocodilian sometimes grows up to 11 feet in length.

Black Caiman

Measuring up to 20 feet long, the black caiman
is the biggest crocodilian in South America.
It lives in the vast Amazon River basin.

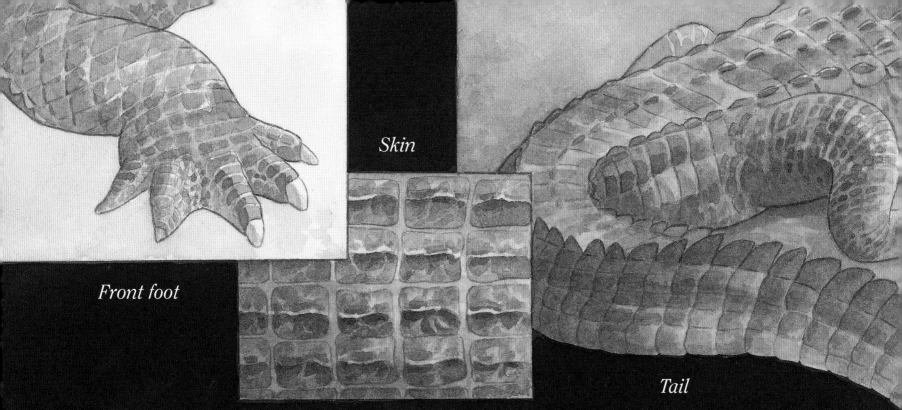

Front foot

Skin

Tail

   All crocodilians are alike in some ways. They all have short legs and clawed feet. They all have long, powerful tails that push their bodies through the water. They all have tough, scaly skins that protect their bodies, much like armor.

   Crocodilians do differ, however, and scientists who study them can tell different species apart. They notice different eye color, body color, and patterns of bumps on the reptiles' backs. They look at the shape of the animals' heads, including the snouts.

   In North America, people often wonder how to tell an American alligator from an American crocodile. The shape of their heads is an important clue. A crocodile's head is narrower than an alligator's. Its snout is more pointed. An alligator's head is broader, and its nose is more rounded than a crocodile's. In addition, the alligator's nostrils are separated by a band of skin while the

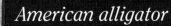

American alligator

When an alligator closes its mouth, only its top teeth are visible. Its lower teeth are hidden. When a crocodile closes its mouth, most of both the upper and lower teeth can be seen. Near the front of an American crocodile's narrow snout, a big tooth on each side of its lower jaw fits into a slot in its upper jaw.

Nostrils very close together

American crocodile

Gharial

All crocodilians are predators. They catch and eat animals, so they have plenty of sharp teeth, at least sixty in number. The gharial has more than one hundred sharply pointed teeth, all about the same size—ideal for grabbing and holding slippery fish, a gharial's favorite food.

When an alligator or other crocodilian loses a tooth, a new tooth soon pushes out to replace it. New teeth keep growing, year after year. In its life—which may last thirty or more years—a crocodilian can have thousands of teeth.

Crocodilians do not chew their food. They swallow animals, or parts of animals, in one gulp. They toss their heads back so the food falls down their throats. When it catches a fish, an alligator or other crocodilian may toss it in the air a few times until the fish can be swallowed headfirst. This keeps the sharp spines on the fish's fins from harming the alligator.

All crocodilians have powerful muscles that enable them to clamp their jaws shut. The muscles that open the jaws are not nearly as strong. All crocodilians also have a big fleshy flap of skin at the back of their mouths. It acts as a valve, closing when the crocodilian opens its mouth underwater. This allows the crocodilian to catch or hold food without swallowing any water.

Alligators and other crocodilians usually breathe through their nostrils. When they dive underwater, muscles close the nostrils so they are watertight. No water gets into the crocodilian's lungs. Once a crocodilian is underwater, its heartbeat slows. Tiny muscles cause some blood vessels to narrow. The flow of blood slows, and so the reptile uses less oxygen. Minute after minute, the crocodilian holds its breath. Even the largest crocodile or alligator can stay underwater for more than an hour.

Alligator tossing fish

Throat flap closed

17

Johnston's crocodile

When an alligator crawls ashore on its belly, it looks slow and awkward, but it can move quickly on land. Alligators and other crocodilians can rise up on their four legs and walk. They can even trot, and small crocodilians can gallop as fast as ten miles an hour for a short distance. With a sudden burst of speed, they can escape danger, or surprise and catch an animal to eat.

Crocodilians catch most of their food in the water. Little bumps on their jaws and bodies contain nerve cells that detect tiny disturbances in the water. This helps them sense the location of a wading bird or a swimming fish or muskrat.

Sensory bumps on snout

Schneider's
dwarf caiman
swimming

Usually crocodilians are ambush predators. They rest patiently in the water and go unnoticed by other animals. Most of the crocodilian's body and head are hidden. Only its nostrils, eyes, and ears are above water, so it can breathe and watch and listen—and wait.

Crocodilians usually swim slowly, paddling with their webbed feet, pushing with side-to-side sweeps of their long, muscular tail. To speed up, they hold their legs tightly against their bodies and swing their tail faster. They can even leap partway out of the water and grab a bird from a branch. Baby crocodilians sometimes snatch dragonflies and other insects from the air.

Soon after hatching, baby alligators and other young crocodilians eat insects, spiders, frogs, and small fish. As they grow bigger, they also hunt for larger prey. The biggest crocodilians catch many fish and also turtles, snakes, birds, and mammals.

Animals that feed along the water's edge or enter the water for a drink are in danger of becoming a crocodilian's meal. American alligators sometimes lunge out of the water to grab a bird, raccoon, or dog. Black caimans catch pigs, small deer, and cattle. Indopacific crocodiles prey on monkeys that hunt for crabs along the water's edge. These big crocodiles also catch wallabies, cattle, horses, and buffalo.

Once in a crocodilian's powerful jaws, an animal is dragged underwater and held there until it drowns. Since crocodilians do not chew their food, they occasionally swallow stones, and even bottles and cans, with their meals.

Crocodilians have small brains, but they are wise in ways of catching food. Caimans and crocodiles sometimes wait in the water beneath the nests of birds or under branches where colonies of fruit bats rest. They have learned that food may flutter or fall within reach. Crocodiles may also line up in the water, forming a barrier that keeps fish from escaping. This makes it easier for the whole "team" to catch food.

In Africa, herds of zebras and wildebeests must cross rivers when they migrate. Nile crocodiles remember the river-crossing places and usually wait there. Once a wildebeest or other large animal is caught, crocodiles take turns feeding. While one crocodile tears off some meat, several others hold the carcass steady in the water.

Most crocodilians never harm humans. American alligators rarely attack people, even though they live in lakes, ponds, canals, and marshes visited and used by millions of people. Compared with alligators and caimans, crocodiles are more aggressive toward humans. Both the Nile and Indopacific crocodile are known to ambush swimmers and even attack small boats.

Nile crocodile
attacking wildebeests

23

A wall carving of the Egyptian god Sobek

Crocodile-headed carving from Papua New Guinea

Example of a Chinese dragon

*Australian Aboriginal
rock painting of a crocodile*

Wherever crocodilians once lived, from Australia to Africa, they appeared in the paintings and wood carvings of ancient peoples and were reflected in societies' beliefs. The Mayans and Aztecs of South America believed that their known world lay on the back of a huge reptile—either a caiman or crocodile—in a pond. In parts of Papua New Guinea, people believed that the Indopacific crocodile created Earth and all of its life.

People of ancient Egypt worshipped more than four hundred gods, but one of the greatest was Sobek, the crocodile god. He was pictured with a human body and a crocodile head. Egyptians built temples for Sobek. At one temple called Crocodilopolis, explorers found dead crocodiles preserved as mummies.

The Chinese alligator is called *tulong*, which means "earth dragon." Historians believe that legends about dragons can be traced back to human experiences with alligators and crocodiles. After explorers from Europe met huge Nile crocodiles, they returned home with reports of these dangerous reptiles. Most people like scary stories, so they used a little information about real crocodilians and imagined mythical dragons.

Alligators bellowing

Make-believe dragons gave mighty roars, and so do real alligators and most other crocodilians—the noisiest reptiles on Earth. Hatchlings croak, grunt, and yelp while still in their eggs. Adults can give hisses and low growls or thunderous roars and bellows. Of all crocodilians, the American alligator is the most vocal. The roar of one animal causes others to join in.

Springtime is mating time in alligator country. Both males and females join in a roaring chorus in the early morning and again in the late afternoon. When courting, the male and female alligators make soft coughs and purring sounds to each other.

Gharial digging its nest

As eggs develop inside the body of a female crocodilian, she builds a nest. Most crocodiles lay their eggs in holes they dig in the ground with their hind feet. They cover the eggs with soil. The warmth of sunlight on the soil helps the young develop inside their eggs. Mother crocodiles sometimes leave the nest for a drink of water, but they usually do not eat. While guarding their nests, they may go without food for ninety days.

Gharials dig nest holes in sandy riverbanks. Caimans and alligators make nests aboveground, piling up soil, branches, and leaves. Eggs are laid in the hollowed-out center of the mound, then covered. As the leaves and other plant parts decay, they give off heat, which helps warm the eggs.

The temperature of the eggs during their early weeks in the nest has a surprising effect. If the temperature is 86 degrees Fahrenheit or lower, females will hatch from the eggs. If it is 94 degrees or above, the hatchlings will be males. Sometimes the eggs closest to the top get quite warm and produce males, while females hatch from the lower, and cooler, eggs.

*Alligator building
its nest mound*

*Alligator
snapping turtle
stalking
alligator
hatchlings*

Even before hatching, baby alligators call to one another in their eggs. If one taps on the inside of its egg, others nearby tap on theirs. Once free of their eggshells, the hatchlings stay close together, often resting in clusters. If they make distress yelps, their mother and sometimes other adult alligators rush to their defense.

A newly hatched alligator weighs only about two ounces and measures eight inches long. It must live for about nine years to reach a length of six feet. Then it's ready to mate and to help produce a new generation of alligators.

Many young alligators and other crocodilians live less than a year. Despite their mothers' defense, they are eaten by all sorts of predators: fish, snakes, herons, snapping turtles, otters, and raccoons. In South America, jaguars kill crocodiles, and even medium-sized caimans can be squeezed to death by anacondas.

Anaconda squeezing a caiman

As the hunted or as hunters, crocodilians are an important part of many food webs. In the Florida Everglades, alligators play another vital role. With their clawed feet, they dig small ponds, three or four feet deep and up to thirty feet wide. Year after year, alligators maintain these ponds. In the dry season or when drought strikes, the ponds help both young and old alligators survive. As the only water in a dried-out marsh, the ponds also help fish, frogs, insects, crabs, birds, and countless other animals stay alive until the rains return.

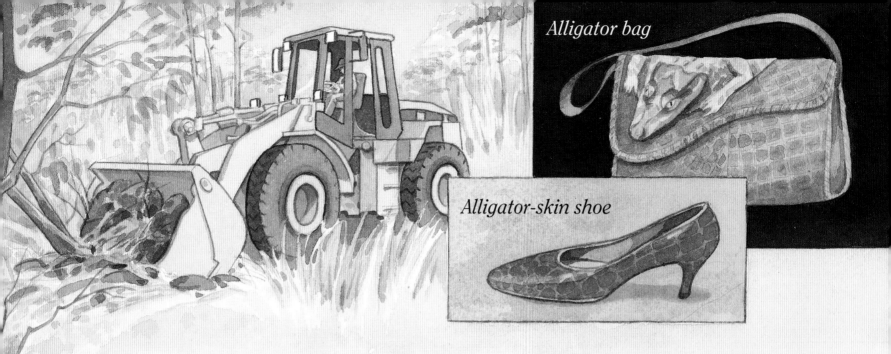

Alligator bag

Alligator-skin shoe

Alligators and other crocodilians are valuable as part of nature, but some people value them in other ways—as a source of food or income. Crocodilian hides are made into shoes, belts, luggage, and handbags. The preserved heads of hatchlings are sold as key-chain rings in novelty stores. Countless millions of crocodilians have been killed to produce these products. Crocodilians also die when wetlands are drained or filled in, which destroys their habitats.

Several crocodilian species are threatened with extinction. Fewer than two hundred Chinese alligators and the same number of Philippine crocodiles exist in the wild. Only a few thousand gharials survive. Alligators thrive in the United States, and regulated hunting is allowed, but action is needed to save some other species around the world.

Crocodilians outlived the dinosaurs and have survived millions of years of change on Earth. Now the future of these strange and wonderful creatures is in human hands.

More About Crocodilians and Their Conservation

With their size, strength, and eighty sharp teeth, American alligators could kill dozens of people every year, but do not. They and other large crocodilians are at times dangerous, but people can reduce that danger if they follow some safety rules when they're in crocodilian habitat. For example, dogs and small children should stay away from the water's edge. People sometimes invite trouble by feeding wild crocodilians. This causes the reptiles to lose their fear of humans and return to a feeding place, looking for something to eat.

Most crocodilian species are harmless to humans. Many nations have laws aimed to protect these reptiles, but illegal hunting continues. People now raise alligators and other crocodilians in great numbers. Sale of meat and skins from these "farmed" animals helps reduce the killing of their wild relatives. Imitation crocodilian skin, made of plastic, now looks remarkably like real skin, but real skin is still considered the ideal for the "high fashion" market. One way people can help rare crocodilians survive is to stop buying products made from them and encourage others to do the same.

Crocodilians cannot live without marshes, swamps, and other wetland habitats. Several environmental organizations work to protect these wild places. They include the World Wildlife Fund and the Nature Conservancy. Supporting such groups helps not only crocodilians but also the rich variety of life that thrives in wetlands. A good source of information about crocodile natural history and conservation is the Web site hosted by the Crocodile Specialist Group. The group's Web address is www.flmnh.ufl.edu/cnhc/.